DOGS SET VII

PUGGLES

Jill C. Wheeler
ABDO Publishing Company

visit us at
www.abdopublishing.com

Published by ABDO Publishing Company, 8000 West 78th Street, Edina, Minnesota 55439. Copyright © 2008 by Abdo Consulting Group, Inc. International copyrights reserved in all countries. No part of this book may be reproduced in any form without written permission from the publisher. The Checkerboard Library™ is a trademark and logo of ABDO Publishing Company.

Printed in the United States.

Cover Photo: Chelle Rohde Calbert/www.designerdoggies.com
Interior Photos: Chelle Rohde Calbert/www.designerdoggies.com pp. 5, 10, 13, 15, 17, 18, 19, 21; Peter Arnold p. 9; www.raineycreekkennel.com p. 11; Rochelle Baltzer p. 7

Editors: Rochelle Baltzer, Heidi M.D. Elston
Art Direction: Neil Klinepier

Library of Congress Cataloging-in-Publication Data

Wheeler, Jill C., 1964-
 Puggles / Jill C. Wheeler.
    p. cm. -- (Dogs. Set VII)
 Includes index.
 ISBN 978-1-59928-965-6
 1. Puggle--Juvenile literature. I. Title.

 SF429.P92W44 2008
 636.76--dc22

                          2007031509

CONTENTS

Dogs by Design

People have long been looking for the perfect dog. More than 12,000 years ago, humans tamed wolf pups to help them hunt and to protect their camps. Those wolf pups **evolved** into modern dogs. Dogs and wolves belong to the Canidae **family**.

Today, there are hundreds of dog **breeds** to choose from. But, some people are still seeking the perfect match. Fortunately, today's dog breeders have a new answer, designer dogs!

Designer dog breeders do not leave breeding to chance or accident. Instead, they purposely pair up different **purebreds**. The **American Canine Hybrid Club (ACHC)** now registers about 400 purebred to purebred crosses.

Puggles are sweet tempered and make great family pets!

Many people claim designer dogs are healthier than **purebred** dogs. This is because purebred puppies often inherit health problems. Mixing two **breeds** introduces different genes. So, the chances of passing on undesirable genes is lowered.

Puggles are one of the most popular designer dogs. They are created by mating a pug with a beagle.

PUGS

Pugs are one of the oldest dog **breeds**. They were bred in China more than 2,400 years ago. Pugs were bred simply to be human companions.

Among Europe's kings and queens, pugs were favorite pets. A pug is credited with saving the life of Dutch prince William I. England's Queen Victoria loved pugs as well.

In the United States, pugs became popular in the 1880s. They were first registered with the **American Kennel Club** in 1885.

Pugs are friendly, eager-to-please dogs that enjoy playing with their owners. They were bred to be lapdogs, so they like lots of attention. They are especially fond of children.

Pugs have short noses that can cause breathing problems. This feature also makes it hard for them to keep themselves cool. Pugs are not very active. So, they tend to become overweight.

Pugs are equally happy in a small apartment or a spacious country estate.

BEAGLES

Beagles were originally **bred** to hunt rabbits. To help them hunt, beagles developed a keen sense of smell. Most beagles in the United States are descendants of beagles imported from England. In the United States, these dogs first became popular in the 1800s.

Beagles are friendly, social dogs. They tend to be intelligent and energetic. Beagles can be very single-minded, too. Once they find a scent, they will track it without considering anything else.

Beagles were bred to follow their instincts. That means they do not always take orders well. Beagles can gain weight if they are not given room to run or walk. They also tend to bark and howl more than many other breeds.

Beagles are known as escape artists. They will do almost anything to follow an interesting scent.

PUGGLE HISTORY

No one is certain where the first puggles were **bred**. Some people believe the first planned puggles were bred in Oklahoma in the 1990s.

Dog breeder Wallace Havens of Wisconsin was the first to register a **litter** of puggles with the **ACHC**. He also claims to have named the puggle. However, there may have been accidental puggles before either of those events.

Puggles are born blind and deaf. Their eyes open after 12 to 14 days. And, their ears open after about 12 days.

Female beagles make loving mothers.

Today, most puggles come from a female beagle **bred** to a male pug. This is because female pugs have a hard time birthing puppies. Often, a veterinarian must deliver **purebred** pug puppies. Female beagles give birth to their puppies about nine weeks after mating.

PUGGLES

Because puggles are not **purebred** dogs, not all of them look alike. Some puggles strongly resemble beagles. Others have more puglike features. Many puggles look like a combination of the two **breeds**.

Most puggles have a solid build with a thick body. A puggle's legs may be short, like a pug's legs. Or they may be long, like a beagle's legs.

A puggle's eyes usually look more like a beagle's eyes, but not always. Often, a puggle has a wrinkled forehead, a curled tail, and drooping ears. Its nose is usually long, like a beagle's nose.

Puggles are popular because they are small and easy to care for. They are good pets for people living in cities or small apartments.

Puggles live an average of 10 to 15 years.

BEHAVIOR

Puggles may be small. But like beagles, they have a lot of energy. Their beagle background may make them eager for a walk each day to burn off energy. However, their pug background means they are equally happy to plop down for a nap. So, owners should provide their puggle with a soft bed.

Like both beagles and pugs, puggles are very social. This means they prefer being around people. And just like their pug parent, puggles want lots of attention. Puggles usually get along well with other pets in the house, too.

Like beagles, puggles often bark at strangers or unfamiliar animals. They may also howl if they are left alone for too long. However, most puggles bark and howl less than **purebred** beagles.

Puggles are well behaved with children and are very playful.

COATS & COLORS

Puggles have soft, smooth, short-haired coats. They need weekly brushing and combing. Unlike some dogs, puggles shed, or lose, their hair.

Caring for a puggle's coat also requires an occasional bath. Puggles need to have their toenails trimmed. And, it is important to clean their ears. In fact, all floppy-eared dogs should regularly have their ears cleaned to prevent infection.

Puggles can be **fawn**, tan, red, black, or white. Some are a solid color. Others are a mixture of colors. The most common puggle color is fawn with a black mask on the snout.

Coat colors can vary within the same puggle litter.

SIZES

Puggles come in two basic sizes, standard and pocket. Standard puggles stand 13 to 15 inches (33 to 38 cm) tall at the shoulders. As adults, they weigh between 18 and 30 pounds (8 and 14 kg).

Some **breeders** raise pocket puggles. To create smaller puppies, they choose to breed only the smallest parents. Pocket puggles may only weigh between 8 and 17 pounds (4 and 8 kg)!

Some people like puggles because they are small and cute. Others like them because they are not as fuzzy as many small dog breeds.

18

CARE

Both beagles and pugs have a tendency to put on weight. And like pugs, puggles tend to eat too much. Over time, they can become overweight. So, it is important to put out just enough food.

Puggles require regular visits to a veterinarian. As puppies, they need vaccinations to prevent common canine diseases. Puggles also should be **spayed** or **neutered** by six months of age if puppies are not desired.

Puggles may have problems if they get too hot. Their beagle qualities may make them want to run. But their pug qualities make it difficult for them to remain cool while running. So, puggles should stay in cool places during hot weather.

Puggles have more energy than **purebred** pugs. They need a fenced yard or long walks on a leash. Beagles want to roam. Yet pugs are not very good at finding their way home. Puggles may wander off and get lost. So, puggle owners must keep a close eye on their pets.

Puggles need a high-quality diet, fresh water, and a collar that contains identification tags.

GLOSSARY

American Canine Hybrid Club (ACHC) - an organization that recognizes all hybrid dogs produced from purebred ancestry. The ACHC keeps track of parentage and ancestry of these dogs.

American Kennel Club - an organization that studies and promotes interest in purebred dogs.

breed - a group of animals sharing the same appearance and characteristics. A breeder is a person who raises animals. Raising animals is often called breeding them.

evolve - to develop gradually.

family - a group that scientists use to classify similar plants or animals. It ranks above a genus and below an order.

fawn - a light grayish brown color.

litter - all of the puppies born at one time to a mother dog.

neuter - to remove a male animal's reproductive organs.

purebred - an animal whose parents are both from the same breed.

spay - to remove a female animal's reproductive organs.

WEB SITES

To learn more about designer dogs, visit ABDO Publishing Company on the World Wide Web at **www.abdopublishing.com**. Web sites about designer dogs are featured on our Book Links page. These links are routinely monitored and updated to provide the most current information available.

INDEX